A NOTE TO PARENTS AND TEACHERS

Smithsonian Readers were created for children who are just starting on the amazing road to reading. These engaging books support the acquisition of reading skills, encourage children to learn about the world around them, and help to foster a lifelong love of books. These high-interest informational texts contain fascinating, real-world content designed to appeal to beginning readers. This early access to high-quality books provides an essential reading foundation that students will rely on throughout their school career.

The four levels in the Smithsonian Readers series target different stages of learning abilities. Each child is unique; age or grade level does not determine a particular reading level. See the inside back cover for complete descriptions of each reading level.

When sharing a book with beginning readers, read in short stretches, pausing often to talk about the pictures. Have younger children turn the pages and point to the pictures and familiar words. And be sure to reread favorite parts. As children become more independent readers, encourage them to share the ideas they are reading about and to discuss ideas and questions they have. Learning practice can be further extended with the quizzes after each title and the included fact cards.

There is no right or wrong way to share books with children. You are setting a pattern of enjoying and exploring books that will set a literacy foundation for their entire school career. Find time to read with your child, and pass on the amazing world of literacy.

Adria F. Klein, Ph.D.
Professor Emeritus
California State University, San Bernardino

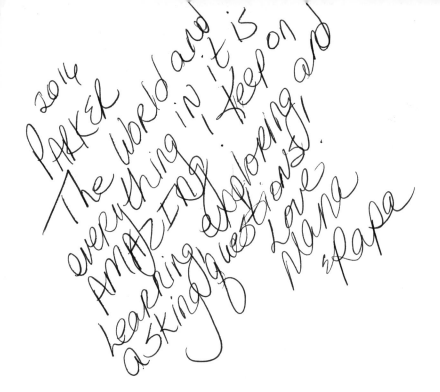

2014
Parker
The world and
everything in it is
AMAZING! I keep on
learning, exploring and
asking questions!
Love
Nana
& Papa

Smithsonian

READERS

Read with Me!

PRE–LEVEL 1

Under the Sea

Planes,
Trains,
and Trucks

Adorable
Baby
Animals

Life on a Farm

What's the
Weather
Outside?

Bodies

Silver Dolphin Books
An imprint of Printers Row Publishing Group
10350 Barnes Canyon Road, Suite 100, San Diego, CA 92121
www.silverdolphinbooks.com

Printers Row Publishing Group is a division of Readerlink Distribution Services, LLC. The Silver Dolphin Books name and logo are trademarks of Readerlink Distribution Services, LLC.

ISBN: 978-1-62686-571-6
Manufactured, printed, and assembled in Dongguan City, China.
19 18 17 16 15   1 2 3 4 5

Adorable Baby Animals; Life on a Farm; and *Under the Sea*
   written by Courtney Acampora
Planes, Trains, and Trucks; Bodies; and *What's the Weather Outside?*
   written by Kaitlyn DiPerna
Cover design by Jenna Riggs
Cover production by Rusty von Dyl
Book design by Kat Godard
Reviewed by Dr. Don E. Wilson, Curator Emeritus of the Department of Vertebrate
   Zoology, National Museum of Natural History, Smithsonian

For Smithsonian Enterprises:
Kealy Gordon, Product Development Manager, Licensing
Ellen Nanney, Licensing Manager
Brigid Ferraro, Vice President, Education and Consumer Products
Carol LeBlanc, Senior Vice President, Education and Consumer Products
Chris Liedel, President

HOW TO USE THIS BOOK

Glossary

As you read each title, you will see words in **bold letters**. More information about these words can be found in the glossary at the end of each title.

Quizzes

Multiple-choice quizzes are included at the end of each title. Use these quizzes to check your understanding of the topic. Answers are printed at the end of the quiz, or you can reread the title to check your answers.

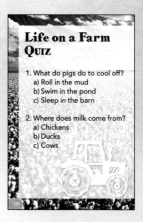

Fact Cards

Each title comes with six tear-out fact cards. Read the cards for fun or use them as quizzes with a friend or family member. You'll be impressed with all you can learn!

ABOUT THE SMITHSONIAN

Founded in 1846, the Smithsonian is the world's largest museum and research complex, consisting of 19 museums and galleries, the National Zoological Park, and nine research facilities. The Smithsonian's vision is to shape the future by preserving our heritage, discovering new knowledge, and sharing our resources with the world.

SMITHSONIAN READER SERIES

Pre–Level 1
Read with Me!

Adorable Baby Animals

Under the Sea

Planes, Trains, and Trucks

What's the Weather Outside?

Life on a Farm

Bodies

Level 1
Early Adventures

Animal Habitats

Outer Space

Reptiles

Vehicles

Safari Animals

Insects

Level 2
Seriously Amazing

Nighttime Animals

Solar System

Baby Animals

Human Body

Dinosaurs and Other Prehistoric Creatures

Sea Life

Level 3
World of Wonder

Sharks!

Wild Weather

Rain Forest Animals

The United States

The Planets

Ancient Egypt

Level 4
Endless Explorations

The Science and History of Flight

Space Exploration

Natural Disasters

World Wonders

Ocean Habitats

Predators

CONTENTS

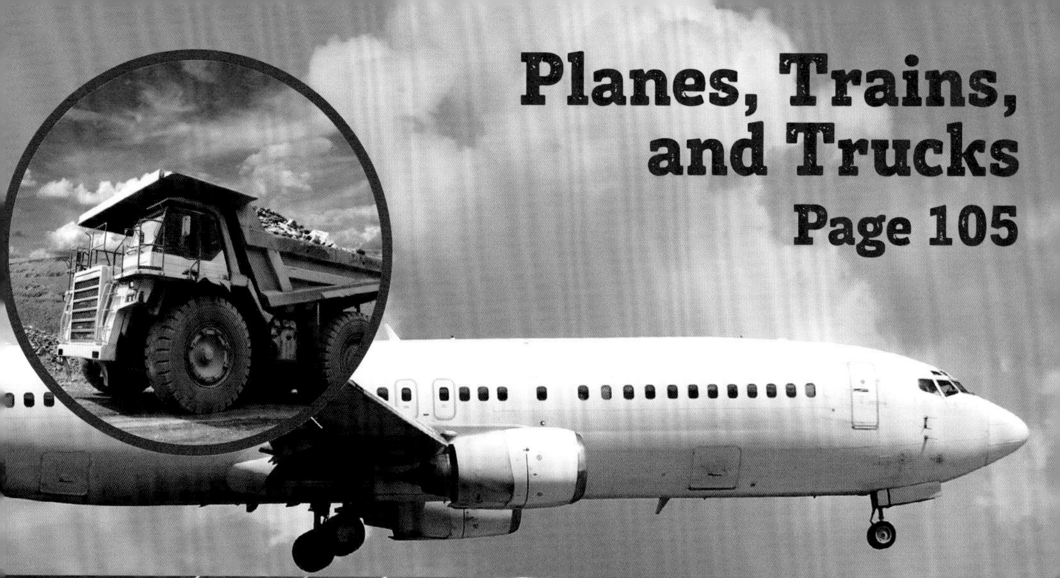

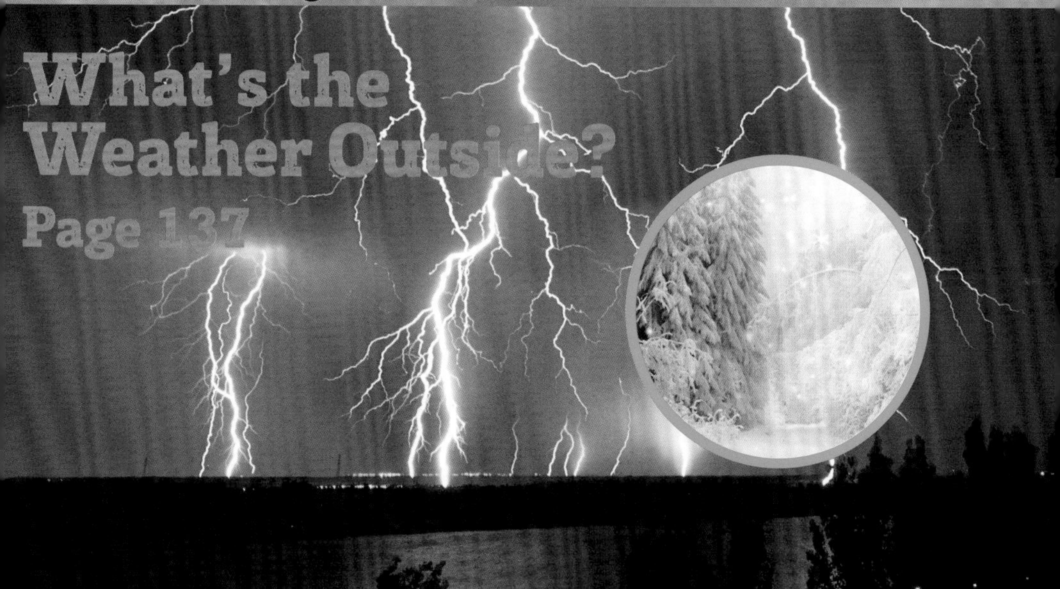

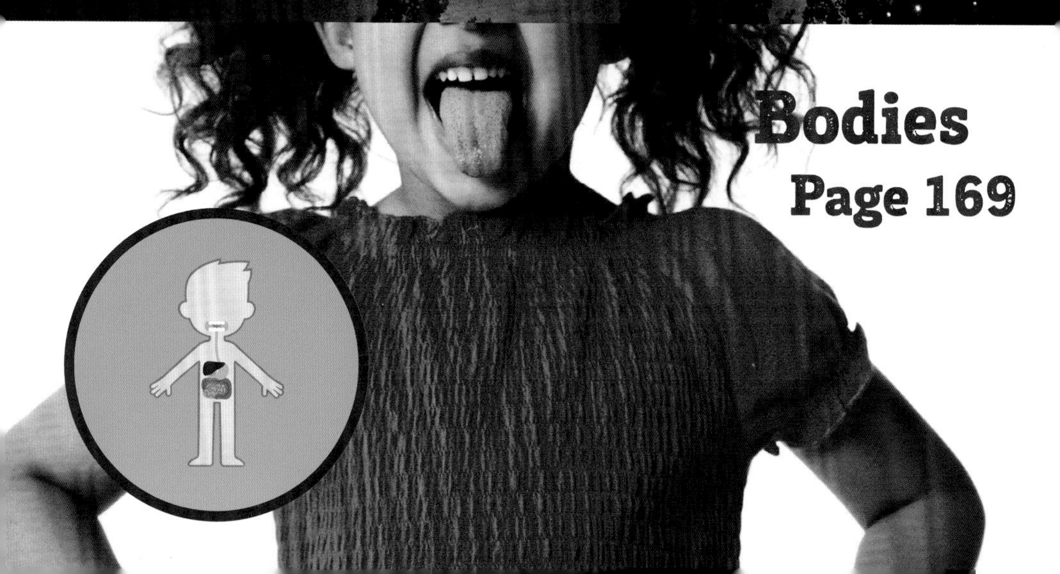

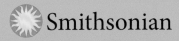
Adorable Baby Animals

Courtney Acampora

Contents

Baby Animals

There are all kinds of baby animals.

Baby Pandas

Baby pandas are very small when they are born.

The mother panda holds the baby.
The baby panda can fit in her paw!

Baby Dolphins

A baby dolphin is called a calf.

Baby dolphins like to play.
They chase other dolphins.

Baby Giraffes

Baby giraffes are six feet tall at birth.

They can walk when they are only a few hours old!

Baby Owls

Baby owls are called chicks.

Owls are **nocturnal**.
They sleep during the day.
They are awake at night.

Baby Sea Otters

Baby sea otters are called pups. Pups float on their mothers' bellies.

The mothers teach the pups to swim.

Baby Chimpanzees

Baby chimpanzees hold onto their mothers.

They hold tight when their mothers climb trees!

Baby Koalas

Baby koalas are called joeys.

Mother koalas have a pouch on their bellies.

Joeys ride in the pouch!

Baby Elephants

Baby elephants can weigh two hundred pounds!

Baby elephants are clumsy at first. They learn to walk and use their **trunk**.

Baby Sea Turtles

Sea turtle mothers lay eggs on a beach.

Hundreds of baby sea turtles **hatch!**

The babies head into the ocean!

Baby Gorillas

Baby gorillas ride on their mothers' backs.

Baby gorillas share a nest with their mothers.

Baby Bears

Baby bears are called cubs.
Cubs are born in a **den**.

Cubs snuggle against their mother.

Baby Lions

Baby lions are called cubs, too!

They play with other cubs.

Growing Up

Baby animals grow up fast.

Baby animals learn about the world around them!

Baby Animals Quiz

1. What is a baby dolphin called?
   a) A joey
   b) A cub
   c) A calf

2. What does "nocturnal" mean?
   a) Active at night
   b) Active during the day
   c) An animal with a pouch

3. What is a baby koala called?
   a) A joey
   b) A cub
   c) A pup

4. Where are bear cubs born?
   a) A nest
   b) A den
   c) The beach

Answers: 1) c 2) a 3) a 4) b

GLOSSARY

Den: an animal home dug into the earth or in a cave

Hatch: to break out of an egg

Nocturnal: active at night

Trunk: the long nose of an elephant

Sea Turtle

Owl

Koala

Bear

Panda

Sea Otter

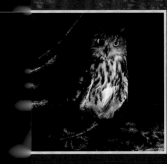

s are nocturnal.

Baby sea turtles hatch from eggs.

Bear cubs are born in a den.

Baby koalas are called joeys.

Otter pups float their mothers' bellies.

Baby pandas are very small when they are born.

Under the Sea

Courtney Acampora

Contents

Earth's Oceans

There are different parts of the **ocean**.

Some are colorful!

Some are cold.
Some are deep.

Tide Pools

Tide pools are **shallow** pools of water by the shore.

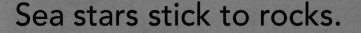

Sea stars stick to rocks.

Crabs scuttle across tide pools.

Sea urchins have sharp spines.

Kelp Forests

Kelp is seaweed that grows tall.

Sea lions swim through kelp forests.

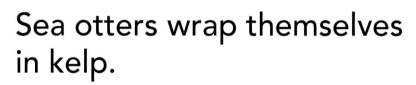

Sea otters wrap themselves in kelp.

Coral Reefs

Colorful fish hide in colorful coral reefs.

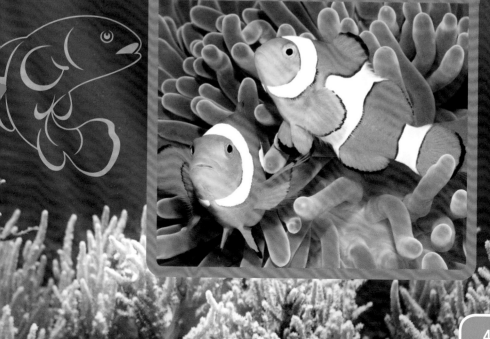

Clown fish are orange with white stripes.

Octopuses have eight arms.

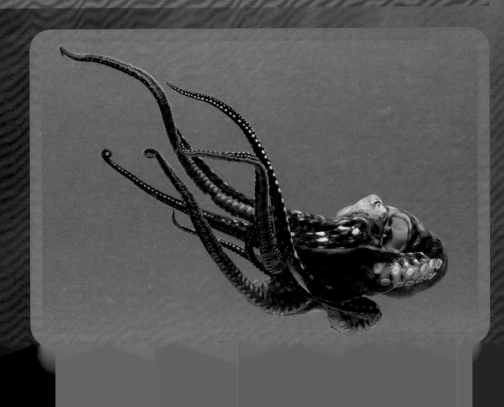

Eels have bodies like snakes.

Sea horse fathers carry their babies before they are born.

Leafy sea dragons look like seaweed.

This helps them blend in.

Lionfish have poisonous fins.

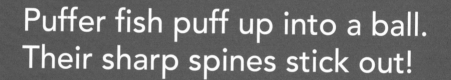

Puffer fish puff up into a ball.
Their sharp spines stick out!

Open Ocean

Big animals swim in the open ocean.

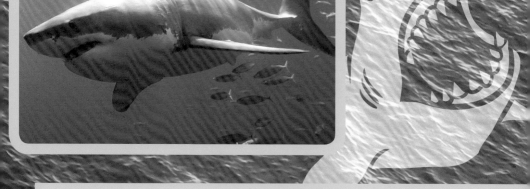

Most sharks have sharp teeth.

Whales are the largest ocean animals.

Whales sing to each other!

Dolphins are playful animals.
Dolphins whistle, click, and chirp.

Sea turtles swim very far.

Sea turtles lay eggs on a beach.

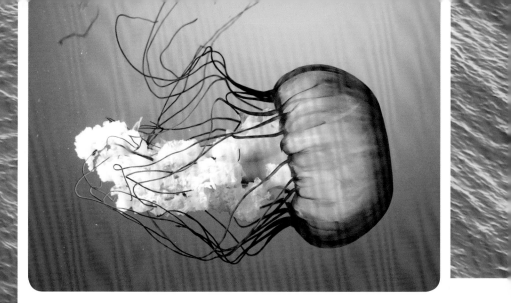

Jellyfish have long, stinging **tentacles**.

Jellyfish do not have brains or bones.

Stingrays have flat bodies and a tail.

Stingrays flap their fins like wings.

Sailfish have large fins on their backs.

They are one of the fastest animals in the ocean!

Icy Waters

Icebergs float in icy waters.

Polar bears' fur keeps them warm in icy waters.

Beluga whales swim in icy waters.

Walruses rest on the ice.

Walruses have long **tusks**.

Penguins are birds.

Penguins use their wings to swim!

Some ocean animals are small.
Some ocean animals are big.

Life is colorful under the sea!

Under the Sea Quiz

1. What is kelp?
   a) Coral
   b) Fish
   c) Seaweed

2. How many arms do octopuses have?
   a) 8
   b) 2
   c) 5

3. What is the largest ocean animal?
   a) Sea urchin
   b) Whale
   c) Eel

4. What animal has tusks?
   a) Stingray
   b) Beluga whale
   c) Walrus

Answers: 1) c 2) a 3) b 4) c

GLOSSARY

Kelp: large seaweed

Ocean: a large body of salt water

Shallow: not deep

Tentacles: flexible limbs

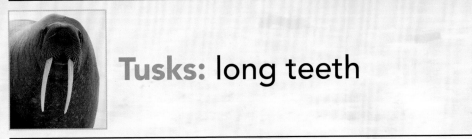

Tusks: long teeth

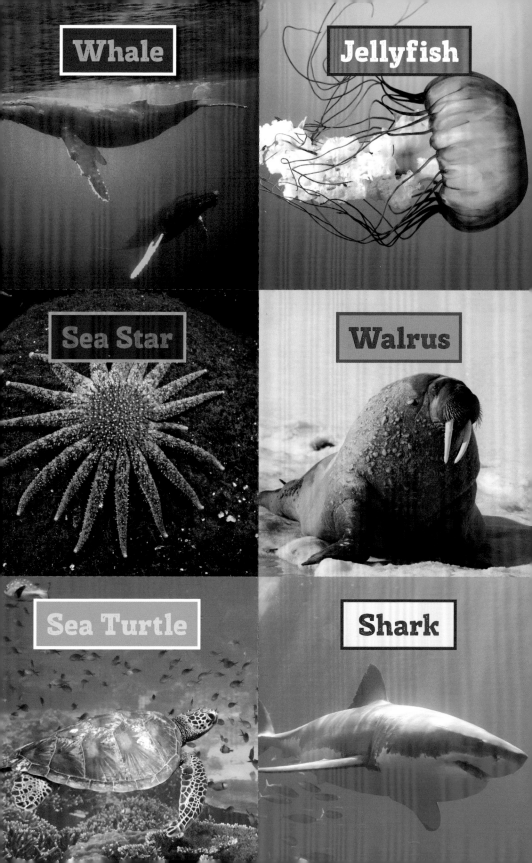

Whale

Jellyfish

Sea Star

Walrus

Sea Turtle

Shark

Jellyfish have long tentacles.

Whales are the largest animals in the ocean.

Walruses have tusks.

Sea stars have many arms.

Sharks are a type of fish.

Sea turtles hatch from eggs.

Smithsonian

Life on a Farm

Courtney Acampora

Contents

Morning on the Farm

The day begins early on the farm.

The rooster crows
"cock-a-doodle-doo!"

Working on the Farm

A farmer works on the farm.

The farmer takes care of the animals and **crops**.

COW

PIGS

SHEEP

LETTUCE

WHEAT

CORN

Crops grow on the farm.

Tractors are used to **harvest** the crops.

Tractors gather hay for the animals to eat.

Tractors drop seeds into the soil.

The seeds grow into plants!

Big Red Barn

The farm has a big red barn.

Animals sleep in the barn.

Horses

The horses say "neigh!"

They eat hay.

Pigs

Pigs live in a pigpen.

They roll in mud to cool off.

Pigs squeak and squeal!

Chickens

Female chickens are called hens.

Hens lay eggs.

Chickens peck at seeds on the ground.

Cows

Cows eat grass.

Cows say "moo!"

Cows give us milk.

 Rabbits

Hop, hop!

Rabbits nibble on grass and carrots.

Ducks

Ducklings swim in a pond.

Ducklings follow their mother.

Goats

Goats have hooves.

Young goats are called kids.

Some goats have horns.

Sheep

Sheep graze in the grass.

Sheep grow thick hair called **wool**.

Wool is used to make clothes.

Sheepdogs

Sheepdogs help **herd** the sheep.

The dog barks "woof, woof!"

Life on a Farm

At night, the animals go to the barn.

Tomorrow will be another busy day!

Life on a Farm
Quiz

1. What do pigs do to cool off?
   a) Roll in the mud
   b) Swim in the pond
   c) Sleep in the barn

2. Where does milk come from?
   a) Chickens
   b) Ducks
   c) Cows

3. What are young goats called?
   a) Hens
   b) Kids
   c) Lambs

4. What animals grow wool?
   a) Sheep
   b) Cows
   c) Goats

GLOSSARY

Crops: plants grown on a farm

Harvest: to gather crops

Herd: to move a group of animals

Wool: sheep hair

Farmer

Goats

Crops

Tractor

Sheep

Ducks

Young goats are called kids.

The farmer takes care of the animals and crops.

Tractors harvest fruits and vegetables.

Crops grow on a farm.

Ducklings follow their mothers.

Sheep grow thick hair called wool.

Planes, Trains, and Trucks

Kaitlyn DiPerna

Contents

Planes, Trains, and Trucks

Planes, trains, and trucks all have the same job.

They move people and things.

Planes

Planes fly through the air.

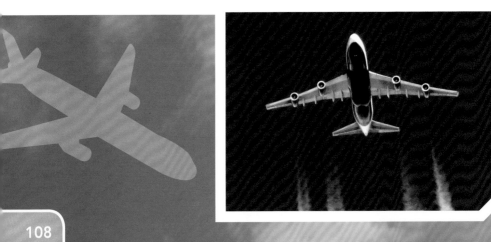

Parts of a Plane

tail

wing

cabin

cockpit

wing

landing gear

Types of Planes

Small planes are flown for fun.

Big planes hold lots of people.

Military planes are fast.

This is a spy plane!

Taking Off and Landing

Planes take off from and land at an airport.

Some military planes use an aircraft carrier!

Planes with pontoons can land on water.

Train wheels roll on tracks.
The tracks are called rails.

Parts of a Train

engine

wheels

rails

Types of Trains

Passenger trains carry people.

Freight trains carry things.

Subways go underground in cities.

Freight trains go across the country.

Train Power

Some trains are powered by **diesel** fuel.

Some trains are powered by electricity.

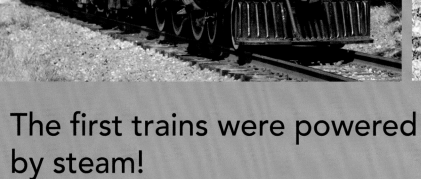

The first trains were powered by steam!

All Aboard!

The **engineer** drives the train.

"All aboard!"

The train pulls out of the station.

"Choo! Choo!"

Trucks

There are all kinds of trucks.

Some trucks move goods.

Some trucks help build roads.

And some trucks help in emergencies.

Parts of Trucks

Semitruck

sleeping space

cab

engine

trailer

wheels

Dump Truck

dumping bed

rock shield

cab

fender

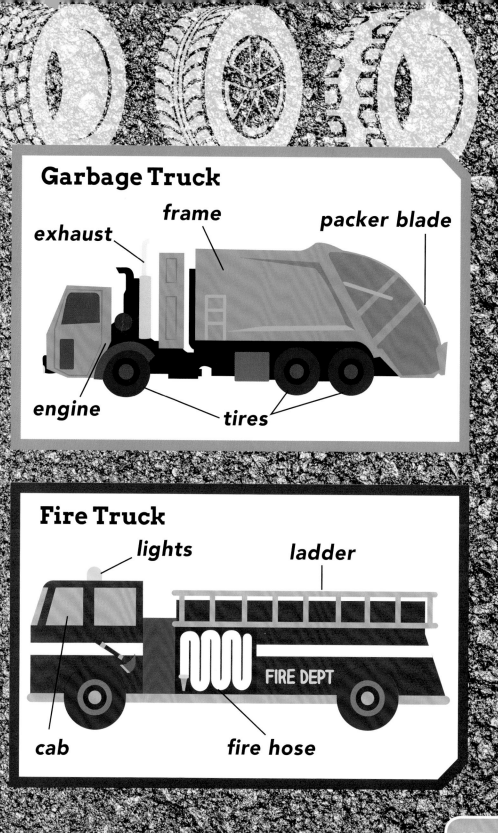

Garbage Truck

exhaust

frame

packer blade

engine

tires

Fire Truck

lights

ladder

cab

fire hose

FIRE DEPT

Semitruck

Semitrucks have a cab in the front.

Semitrucks have a trailer in the back.

The trailer holds goods such as food, toys, or clothes.

Dump Truck

A dump truck has a box at the back called a bed.

The bed can hold rocks, sand, or dirt.

The bed lifts up.

The truck dumps all the rocks, sand, or dirt out!

Garbage Truck

A garbage truck picks up trash.

A garbage truck brings the trash
to a dump or recycling center.

Fire Truck

Fire trucks are used to fight fires.

A pumper truck pumps water from a hydrant.

A ladder truck can reach tall buildings.

A tanker truck has a tank full of water.

Planes, Trains, and Trucks Quiz

1. Planes with pontoons can land where?
   a) On water
   b) On an aircraft carrier
   c) In a field

2. What are train tracks called?
   a) Roads
   b) Rails
   c) Subways

3. How were the first trains powered?
a) Steam
b) Electricity
c) Cars

4. What is the box at the back of a dump truck called?
a) Cab
b) Box
c) Bed

GLOSSARY

Diesel: a type of liquid fuel

Engineer: a person who drives a train

Freight: goods that are shipped

Military: having to do with soldiers or armies

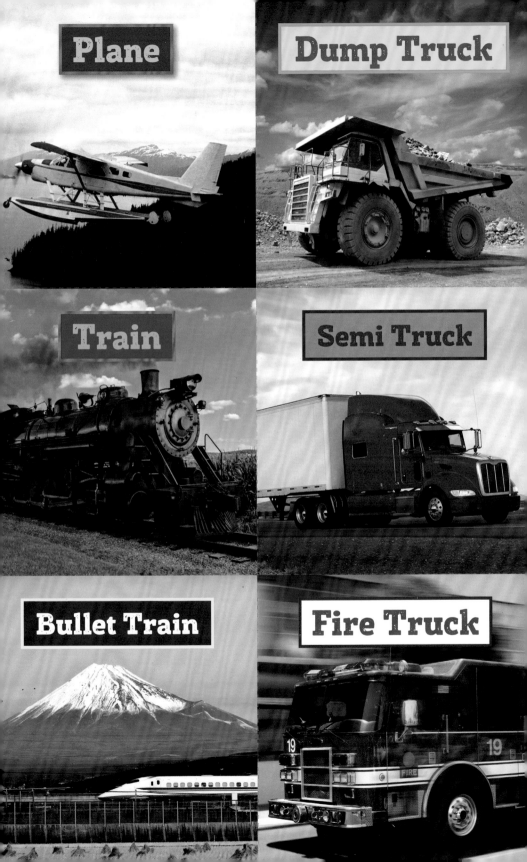

Plane

Dump Truck

Train

Semi Truck

Bullet Train

Fire Truck

A dump truck can hold
rocks, sand, or dirt.

Planes with pontoons
can land on water.

Semi trucks have a
trailer in the back.

Train wheels roll
on rails.

A fire truck carries
water, hoses, and
ladders.

Bullet trains are the
fastest trains.

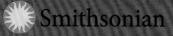
What's the Weather Outside?

Kaitlyn DiPerna

Contents

What Is Weather?

sun

rain

snow

Weather is what it is like outside.

The weather can be bright and sunny.

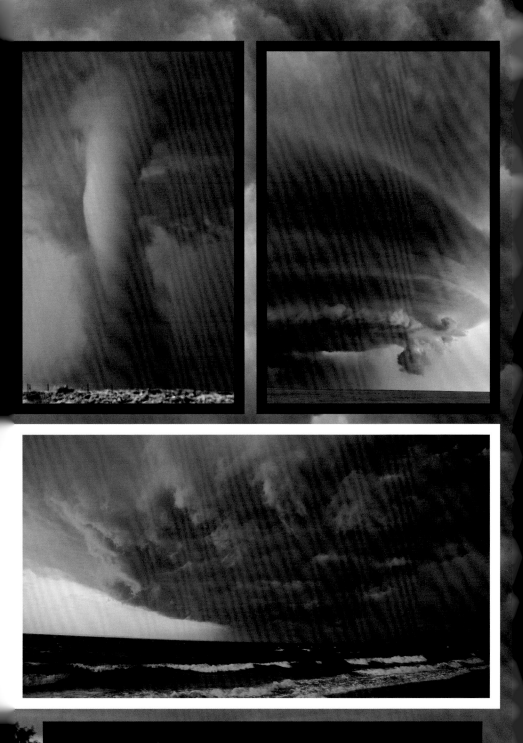

The weather can be dark

What Causes Weather?

The sun causes all of Earth's weather!

The sun's heat causes wind, rain, and snow!

The Seasons

The Earth tilts toward the sun.
Then it is summer.

summer

fall

The Earth tilts away from the sun.
Then it is winter.

winter

spring

The weather is cold in the winter.

The weather warms up in the spring.

The weather is hot in the summer.

The weather cools off in the fall.

Wind

Wind is the movement of air.

Wind can be a light breeze.
Wind can be a powerful gust!

Clouds

Clouds are made of tiny water droplets.

Some clouds are long and thin. Some clouds are tall and fluffy.

cirrus clouds

stratus clouds

cumulus clouds

cumulonimbus clouds

Rain

Water droplets in clouds can grow heavy.

Then they fall as rain.

Rain fills lakes, rivers, and oceans.

People, plants, and animals need water to drink.

Rainbows

Sunlight passes through tiny water droplets in the air.

A rainbow is formed!

There are seven colors in a rainbow.

red

orange

yellow

green

blue

indigo

violet

Floods

Too much rain causes a flood.

Floods can wash away roads, cars, and houses!

Thunderstorms

Thunderstorms have tall, dark, fluffy clouds.

boom!

Thunderstorms bring rain and wind.

Thunderstorms bring lightning and thunder too!

Tornadoes

Tornadoes are powerful windstorms with spinning clouds.

Tornadoes come from thunderstorms.

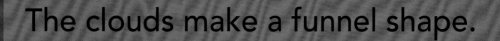

The clouds make a funnel shape.

Tornadoes can knock down trees and destroy houses!

Hurricanes

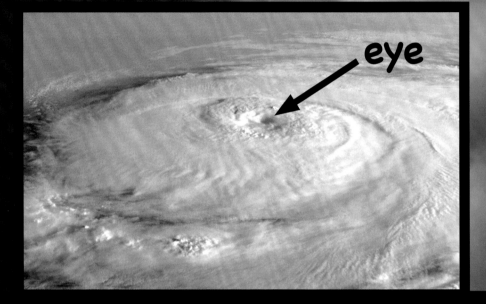

eye

Hurricanes are very strong storms.
Hurricane clouds spin around
an eye.

Hurricanes bring wind, rain, and big waves.

Snow

Snowflakes are made of ice crystals.

No two snowflakes are the same!

Big snowstorms are called **blizzards.**

What's the Weather Outside? Quiz

1. What causes Earth's weather?
   a) The wind
   b) The sun
   c) The oceans

2. What are clouds made of?
   a) Water droplets
   b) Rainbows
   c) Wind

3. How many colors are in a rainbow?
   a) Five
   b) Twelve
   c) Seven

4. What kind of clouds do thunderstorms have?
   a) Tall, dark, fluffy clouds
   b) Long, thin clouds
   c) Tornado clouds

Answers: 1) b 2) a 3) c 4) a

GLOSSARY

Blizzards: big snowstorms

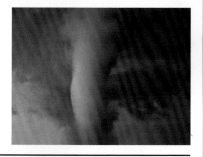

Hurricanes: very strong storms that bring wind, rain, and waves

Tornadoes: funnel-shaped clouds that spin very fast

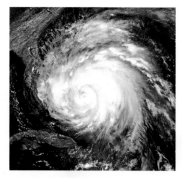

Weather: the conditions outside

Blizzard

Tornado

Hurricane

Thunderstorm

Rainbow

Clouds

Tornadoes are strong windstorms with spinning funnel clouds.

Blizzards are big snowstorms.

Thunderstorms bring rain, thunder, and lightning.

Hurricanes are big storms that bring wind, rain, and waves.

Clouds are made of tiny water droplets.

Rainbows are made when sunlight passes through water droplets in the air.

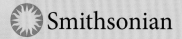

Smithsonian

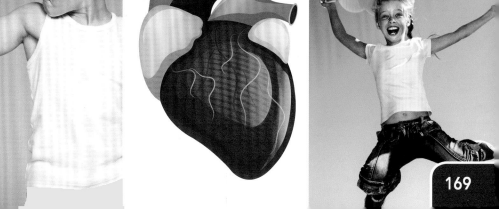

Bodies

Kaitlyn DiPerna

169

Contents

Bodies

animal body

insect body

human body

Bodies come in all shapes and sizes.

Inside and Out

On the outside, human bodies look different.

On the inside, human bodies look the same!

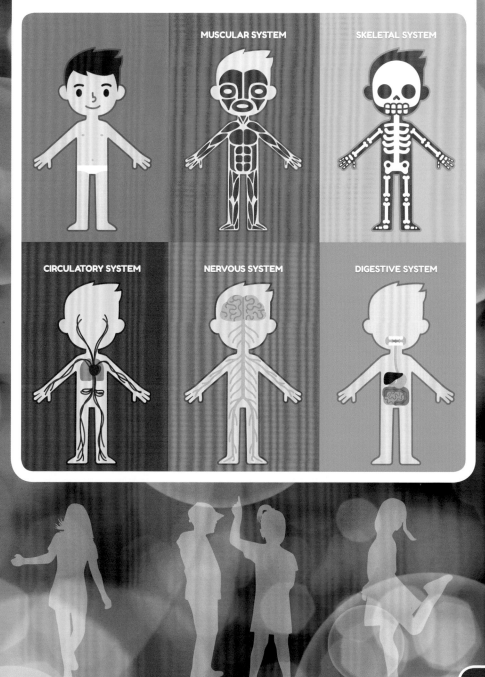

MUSCULAR SYSTEM

SKELETAL SYSTEM

CIRCULATORY SYSTEM

NERVOUS SYSTEM

DIGESTIVE SYSTEM

Your body is made of tiny **cells**.

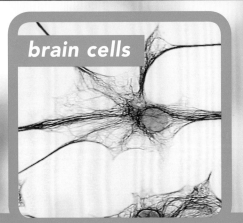

brain cells

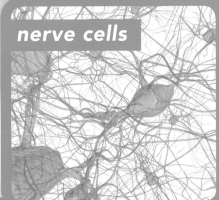

nerve cells

Different cells have different jobs.

Your body contains trillions of cells!

Skin covers your body.

Hair grows out of skin.

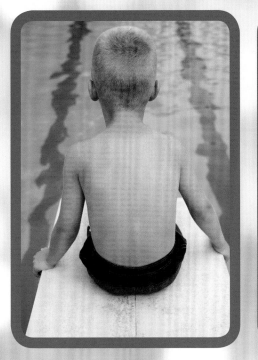

Skin and hair come in lots of different colors.

Bones

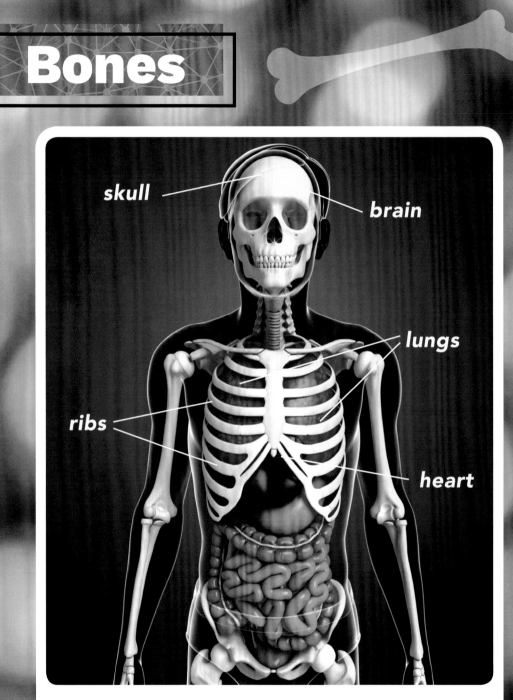

skull

brain

lungs

ribs

heart

Bones help you move.
Bones protect your **organs**.

Your body has two hundred and six bones!

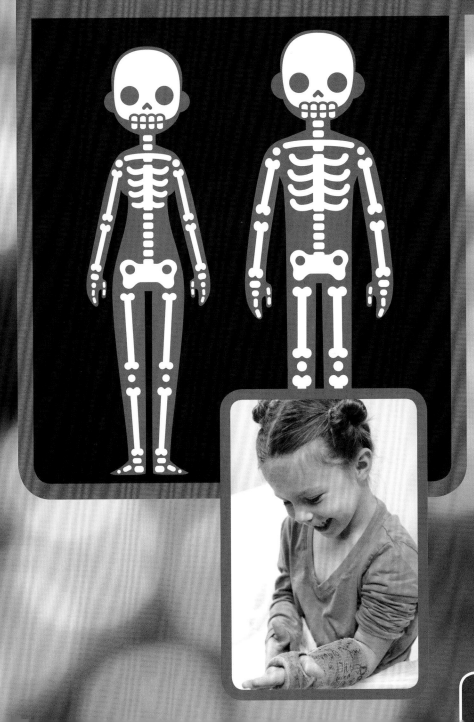

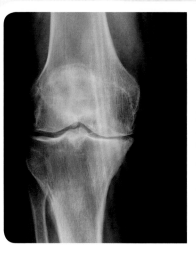
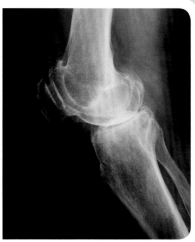

A joint is where two bones come together.

A joint lets you move and bend.

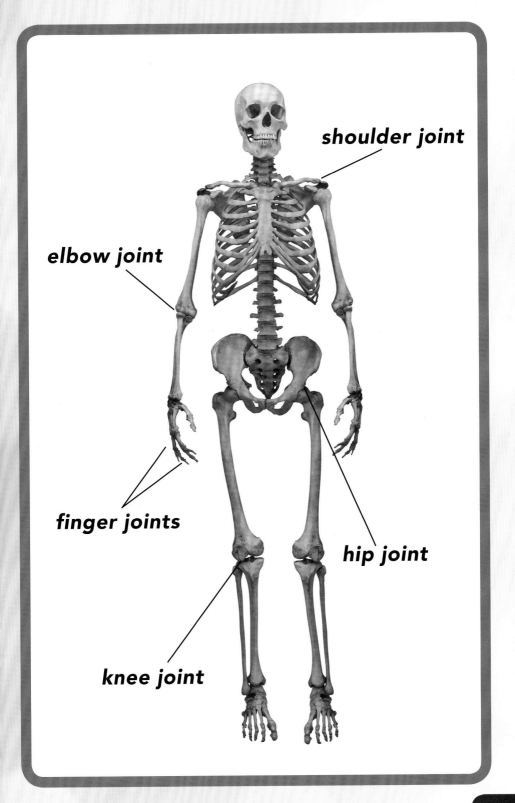

shoulder joint

elbow joint

finger joints

hip joint

knee joint

Muscles

Some muscles you control.

Some muscles work without your help.

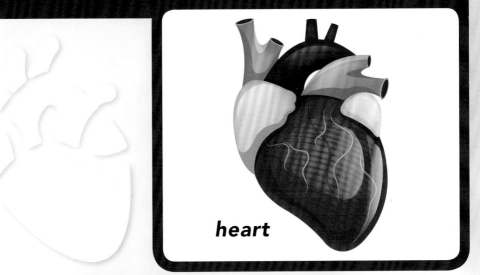

heart

Your body has about six hundred and fifty muscles!

Breathing

Your body gets **oxygen** from the air you breathe.

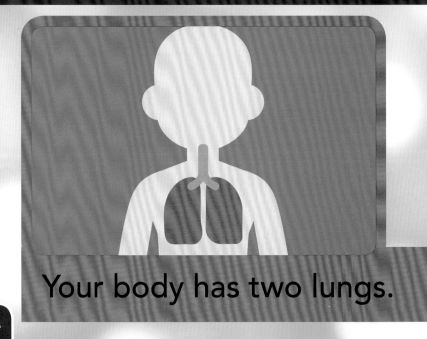

Your body has two lungs.

When you breathe in, your lungs fill with oxygen.

Heart and Blood

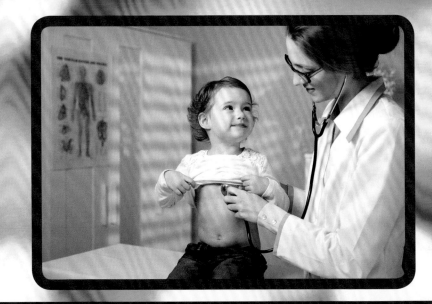

Your heart pumps blood through your body.

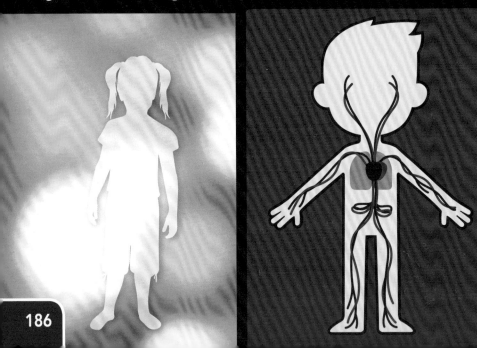

Blood carries oxygen.

Your brain is a very important organ.

Your brain works faster than a computer!

Your brain controls everything you feel, think, and do.

The Five Senses

You have five main **senses**.

sight

hearing

Your senses tell you about the world around you.

smell

taste

touch

Feeding Your Body

Your body needs food.

Food keeps you healthy.

Food gives you energy.

Digestion

Your teeth help you chew food.

Food travels down to your stomach.

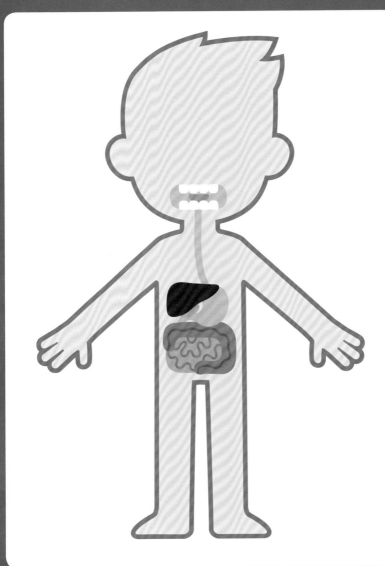

What your body doesn't need comes out as waste.

Keeping Healthy

Keeping your body healthy is important.

Eating healthy foods can keep you from getting sick.

Exercise keeps your muscles and heart strong.

Bodies Quiz

1. What do your bones protect?
   a) Your organs
   b) Your skin
   c) Your blood

2. What do your joints do?
   a) Protect your organs
   b) Keep your muscles and
      heart strong
   c) Let you move and bend

3. What does your heart do?
   a) Gives you energy
   b) Pumps blood through
      your body
   c) Tells you about the world
      around you

4. How many main senses do
   you have?
   a) Five
   b) Two
   c) Eight

GLOSSARY

Cells: tiny building blocks that form living things

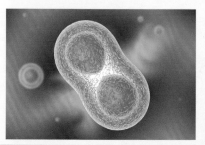

Organs: parts of the body that have a job to do

Oxygen: a gas we breathe

Senses: sight, hearing, smell, taste, and touch

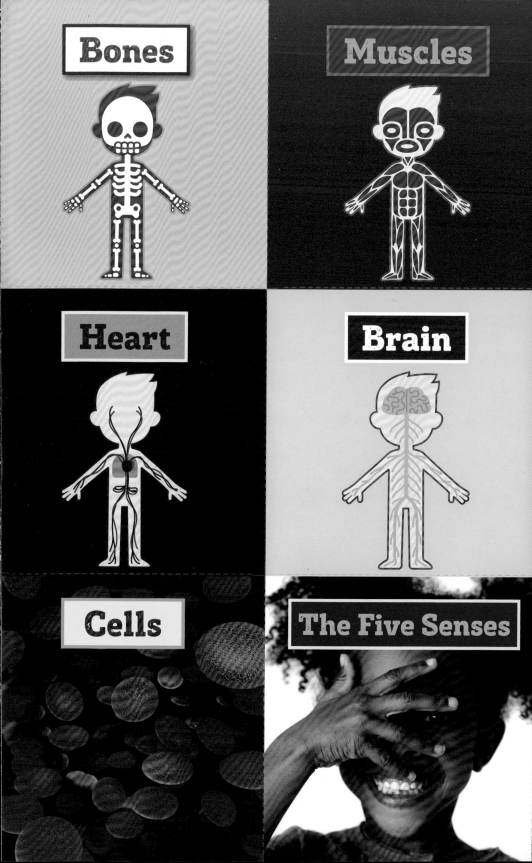

Bones

Muscles

Heart

Brain

Cells

The Five Senses

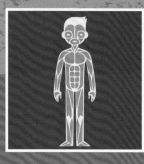

Some muscles you control. Some muscles work without your help.

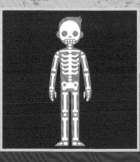

Your body has two hundred bones!

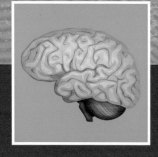

Your brain controls everything you feel, think, and do.

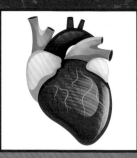

Your heart pumps blood through your body.

Taste   Hearing   Smell

Sight   Touch

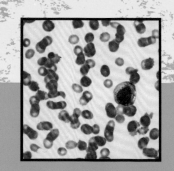

Your body is made of trillions of cells!

LEVEL GUIDELINES

PRE–LEVEL 1: ASPIRING READERS

- Content designed for reading with support from a parent or caregiver
- Short and simple informational texts with familiar themes and content
- Concepts in text are reinforced by photos
- Introduces glossaries with pictorial support
- Simple sentence structure and repeated sentence patterns
- Easy vocabulary familiar to kindergarteners and first-graders

LEVEL 1: EARLY READERS

- Basic factual texts with familiar themes and content
- Concepts in text are reinforced by photos
- Includes glossary to reinforce reading comprehension
- Phonic regularity
- Simple sentence structure and repeated sentence patterns
- Easy vocabulary familiar to kindergarteners and first-graders

LEVEL 2: DEVELOPING READERS

- Simple factual texts with mostly familiar themes and content
- Concepts in text are supported by images
- Includes glossary to reinforce reading comprehension
- Repetition of basic sentence structure with variation of placement of subjects, verbs, and adjectives
- Introduction to new phonic structures
- Integration of contractions, possessives, compound sentences, and some three-syllable words
- Mostly easy vocabulary familiar to kindergarteners and first-graders